Yankee
WEATHER PROVERBS

Yankee
WEATHER PROVERBS

EDITED BY
PETER MILLER

ILLUSTRATIONS BY
DARYL V. STORRS

Daryl V. Storrs

SILVER PRINT PRESS
COLBYVILLE, VERMONT

Dedicated to Vagaries

Library of Congress Control Number: 2004094043
ISBN: 0-9749890-0-2
Dewey Call Number: 551.6
Name: Peter Miller, Editor/Foreword; Daryl V. Storrs, Illustrator
Title: Yankee Weather Proverbs
Publication: First Edition, 2004
Published: Colbyville, VT; Silver Print Press, 2004
Material: 96 pages, color illustrations;   cm.
Subject:
  1. Weather – New England – Folklore
  2. Weather Forecasting – New England
  3. Proverbs

Book Design by Peter Holm, Sterling Hill Productions.
Printed in Singapore

FIRST EDITION

FOREWORD

There's an old saying in northern New England: "If you don't much like the weather, wait five minutes." This country cliché is, of course, completely false. The weather does not change in five minutes. To go from clear blue sky to solid cloud cover takes at least half an hour. A fifty- or sixty-degree change in temperature needs a little longer. Overnight even.

An interesting phenomenon about Yankee weather is that the published and broadcasted weather reports are often as wrong as snow on the Fourth of July, particularly in the spring and the fall. Trust me. As a photographer, I know this. I have heard weather reports of sunny skies while the sky overhead is nothing but a sheet of gray clouds. Conversely, I have listened to reports of overcast skies and, at the appointed time, seen nary a cloud. Encouraged by a sunny sky weather report, I have driven more than sixty miles to take a photograph, then set up my tripod only to look up and see a long line of clouds overrunning and extinguishing the sun. This has happened more often than I care to think about. Once I even heard a weather forecaster give the wrong date for the full moon!

Don't get me wrong, I love weather forecasters—they are the baseball umpires of the sky. They make the call and if they are wrong they cross their arms, put their nose to the sky, zip shut their mouth, and tough it out. They prove that science can be, well, human.

An up-ended weather forecast is a reminder that human beings are not, and have never been, in control of the wind, rain, sleet, snow, or the beautiful blue skies that can make our existence so exuberant. We can't even predict them.

But we've always tried. Throughout our history and long before satellite weather maps, weather balloons, ground and sea temperature readings, humidity recordings, computer-generated weather models, and instant communication, we Yankees have drawn on personal observation to make sense of the weather.

Collected in these pages are a selection of those humanly wrought observations which, on account of an accuracy greater than the capability of modern science, have become proverbial.

PETER MILLER
Colbyville, Vermont

SPRING

March robin, Devil's warning.

In March much snow,
To plants and trees much woe.

Thunderstorms in March
mean a late spring.

The number of days the last snow remains on
the ground indicates the number of snowstorms
that will occur the following winter.

Plant corn if the wind is in the
south on the first day of spring.
Plant wheat if the wind is in the north.

March comes in like a lion and goes out like a ram.

When you hear the first frogs of spring,
you may be sure that the frost is out of the ground.

Three frosts after the frogs first sing in the spring
means warm weather.

Frogs singing in the evening
indicate a fair tomorrow.

A cold wet May means a barn full of hay.

Expect a storm when the pond lies flat as glass,
the fish are not rising, and the insects are still.

Thunder in spring, cold will bring.

You may shear your sheep
when the elder blossoms peep.

If spring is cold and wet,
then the autumn will be hot and dry.

If the first thunderstorm in spring is in the south,
it indicates a wet season. If it is in the north,
there will be a dry season.

When the corn is above the crow's back
the frost is over.

Rain on Easter gives slim fodder.

Plant beans when the moon is light,
plant potatoes when the moon is dark.

When the moon lies on her back,
she sucks the wet into her lap.

A change in the moon brings on
a change in the weather.

When butterflies come early in the season,
they mean fair weather.

If it is eighty degrees or above
for three days in a row in spring,
there will be no black flies that summer.

A windy winter means a rainy spring.

Mist in May and heat in June
brings all things into tune.

Rainbow in the eastern sky,
the morrow will be dry.
Rainbow in the west that gleams,
rain falls in streams.

If it rains on Easter Sunday,
it will rain the next seven days.

Waning moon, plant biennials,
perennials, and bulb root crops.

If all the stars are out tonight,
it will be a nice day tomorrow.

Waxing moon, plant annuals that
produce their yield above ground.

When the stars begin to huddle,
the earth will soon become a puddle.

Shear your sheep in May,
and shear them all away.

If it thunders on April Fool's Day,
it brings good crops of corn and hay.

SUMMER

When the moon changes on Saturday,
expect foul weather.

A circle around the moon or sun indicates
a storm within forty-eight hours.
The smaller the circle, the closer the storm.

If you can hang a hunter's powder horn
on the new moon so it won't slip off,
there will be a dry spell.

Expect dry weather when the Big Dipper will hold water, but expect wet weather when it turns over.

If the rooster crows on the fence, it is a sign that the weather is going to change.

When the cows lie down after being turned
out in the morning, it is a sign of rain.

Low banks of haze in the south indicate rain.

Crickets and tree toads singing loudly in the
evening indicate it will be fair and hot.

When the swallows fly high in the evening,
the next day will be fair,
but when they fly low, expect rain.

Unusually bright stars indicate a storm is on the way.

Thunder after midnight means
the next day will be lowery.

When a storm clears off in the night,
soon there will be another storm.

A sundog in the morning means a storm;
two sundogs mean a heavy rain.

Heavy dew at night promises a good day to follow,
but no dew in the morning indicates rain.

When a spider web lies flat on the grass in the
morning, it will be a fair day, but if the webs are
like tents, so the water can run off, it will rain.

When the wind is in the north, the skillful fisher goes not forth; when the wind is in the south, it blows the bait in the fish's mouth; when the wind is in the west, then it is very best; but when the wind is in the east, it blows no good to man or beast.

Rain before seven, clear before eleven.
Rain after seven, rain all day.

Winter fog will freeze a dog;
summer fog will roast a hog.

Three foggy mornings will be followed by rain.

When the fog goes up the mountain hopping,
the rain comes down a-dropping.

If the wind is from the south when the sun crosses
the equinoxes, it will be much warmer, but if the
wind is from the north, beware of cooler weather.

Variable wind indicates a coming storm.

When leaves turn over, it is a sign of rain.

Froth along the shores of streams is a sign of rain.

Whitecaps on the pond or river
signify that it is going to rain.

When the locks turn damp in the
scalp house, rain will come.

If it rains while the sun shines,
it will rain the following day.

A sun drawing water will bring
wind and rain within two days.

If it rains on the first Sunday of the month,
every Sunday except one will be wet.

Still, moist, and damp hot air
means rain is on the way.

A clear day with light winds and balmy
temperatures is a weather breeder.

Sounds that carry far and clear in
the summer mean rain, but in the
winter they mean severe cold.

Sparks on the bottom of the tea kettle
are a sign of rain.

Weak and poor radio reception
means a storm is in the air.

A soggy straw hat indicates rain, but a straw hat
crackly and stiff indicates fair weather.

There will be fair weather if there is enough
blue in the northwestern sky to make
a Scotchman a jacket.

If it rains on the first dog day of August,
it will rain on each of the other nine;
if it is dry the first dog day,
all the rest will be dry.

Red sky at night, sailors delight.
Red sky in morning, sailors take warning.

A storm is coming when the sun
sets with a cloud underneath.

When the robins call loudly and steadily,
it will rain soon.

Cuckoo on the hill brings water to the mill.

If the blue heron flies downstream, it will bring rain; if it flies upstream, it will be fair.

Large numbers of birds roosting
on a wire indicate rain.

When a hen or duck oils its feathers,
it is a sign of rain.

It is a sign of rain when the flies bite.

There will be rain:
  If the rooster flaps his wings.
  If the hogs grunt and are restless.
  If the hens nestle and flutter in the dust.
  If the bees stay close to the hive.

Step on a spider or a beetle
and it will surely bring rain.

When the ants close up their hills,
we will have rain in a day or two.
If the anthills are open,
it will continue to be fair.

If you kill a snake and hang it up, rain will fall.
If you bury it, the weather will be fair.

A cat or dog eating grass
is a warning that a storm is on the way.

An old cat running about and feeling good
is a sign that the wind is going to blow.

If chickens come out while it is raining,
the storm will be a long one;
if they stay under cover, it will be short.

When a thunderstorm threatens,
if cattle go under trees, it will be a shower;
if they continue to feed, it will be continuous rain.

If the cows are lying down, bad weather is coming.

Mackrel sky, mackrel sky —
never long wet, never long dry.

A mare's tail in the sky is a sure sign of rain.

Thunderheads moving from southeast
to northwest indicate rain.

A brassy sky in the west at sunset
is a sign of high winds.

Sunset clear on Friday night,
rain before Monday night.

The temperature in degrees Fahrenheit can be esti-
mated by counting the number of chirps made by a
cricket in fourteen seconds and adding forty.

After seeing lightning, count the seconds until you
hear the thunder, then divide by five. The answer
you get is the number of miles away the storm is.

If June is sunny, the harvest will come early.

The moon, her face if red be, of water speaks she.

Fog from seaward, fair weather;
fog from landward, rain.

When grass is dry at morning light,
look for rain before the night.

When seagulls fly to land, a storm is at hand.

If salt is sticky and gains in weight,
it will rain before too late.

The higher the clouds, the better the weather.

When the smell of ditches offends the nose,
look for rain and stormy blows.

If wooly fleeces deck the heavenly way,
be sure no rain will mar a summer's day.

When the rooster goes crowing to bed,
he will rise with a watery head.

A severe summer foretells a windy autumn.

If the perfume of flowers is especially strong,
rain will come soon.

AUTUMN

Look for frost six weeks after the
katydids chirp in the summer.

When robins leave early,
expect an early winter.

Large flocks of crows flying about
in fall mean a hard winter.

If the hens stop laying, there will be a hard winter
but if the rabbit sits up particularly straight,
there will be a mild winter.

If there is a heavy peel on the onions,
there will be a hard winter.

If a pig dressed in the fall has extra thick pork,
there will be a hard winter.

If the sumac turns too early,
there will be a hard winter.

If the apples fall to the ground in large
quantities rather than a few at a time,
there will be a mild winter.

A thunderstorm in October
is a sign of a long, cold winter.

When the mountains look a beautiful clear lightish blue and rather indistinct, it indicates snow, but if they are dark blue, vivid, and the tree trunks look dark and distinct, it indicates rain. In either case, it will come soon.

If the husks on the corn are heavy and tight,
if apple skin is tough to bite,
there will be a hard winter.

Three white frosts and then a storm.

Big bean crop, bad winter.

When dry leaves rattle on the trees, expect snow.

If the first snow sticks to the trees,
it foretells a bountiful harvest.

The date on which the snow first falls enough
to track a cat determines the number of
snowstorms for the coming winter.

When the first snow remains on the ground
for some time in a place not exposed to the sun,
expect a hard winter.

If the snow remains on the trees in November,
they will bring out but few buds in spring.

Purple or very dark blue clouds indicate snow as do
long flat banks of dark-colored clouds.

If the snowflakes increase in size,
a thaw will follow.

As many days as the snow remains on the trees,
just so many days will it remain on the ground.

A heavy November snow will last until April.

If the oak trees bear many acorns
it foreshadows a long, hard winter.

Observe on what day in August the first
heavy fog occurs, and expect a hard
frost on the same day in October.

When clouds look like black smoke
a wise man will put on his cloak.

If autumn leaves are slow to fall,
prepare for a cold winter.

The first frost in autumn will be exactly six months
after the first thunderstorm of the spring.

Bats flitting about late in the evening in spring
and fall foretell a fine day on the morrow.

When squirrels lay in a big store of nuts,
look for a hard winter.

Clear moon, frost soon.

Fair on September first, fair for the month.

In October, dung your field,
and your land its wealth will yield.

A wide brown band on a wooly bear means a mild
winter. A narrow band means a severe winter.

WINTER

Snow is the poor man's fertilizer — a snowy winter,
a plentiful harvest. A snow year, a rich year.

A green Christmas, a fat graveyard;
a white Christmas, a lean graveyard.

So far as the sun shines on Christmas Day,
so far will the snow blow in May.

If the snow that falls during the winter is dry and is
blown about by the wind, a dry summer will follow;
very damp snow indicates rain in the spring.

Snow is generally preceded by animation of man and
beast, which continues until after the snowfall ends.

If the first heavy snow falls on frozen ground,
it will melt, but if it falls on mud, it will stay.

Snow that comes in the old of the moon is apt to last; snow that comes in the new of the moon soon is past.

If a snowstorm begins when the moon is young, the rising of the moon will clear away the snow.

It takes three cloudy days to bring a heavy snow.

As many days as the snow remains on the trees, just so many days will it remain on the ground.

There will be as many snowstorms during the season as there are days remaining in the month after the time of the first snow.

Northern lights are a sign of cold weather.

When smoke goes straight up from the chimney, look for a storm.

If the wood in the stove burns up quickly, or soot burns off the stove, a storm is on the way; burning wood in the winter pops more before snow.

Expect cold weather if the cat sits on the hearth with its back to the north or if the birds fill up on suet at the feeder.

Deep blue clear skies in the winter mean a very cold day. Purple or very dark blue clouds indicate snow.

Snow can be expected after a prolonged cold spell.

If the snow on the roof or ice on trees
melts off, the next storm will be rain;
but if it blows off, one can reckon on snow.

Heavy white frost on trees and bushes after a cold
spell in the winter signifies that it will rain.

Much sleet in winter will be followed
by a good fruit year.

Cut a snowball in halves; if it is wet inside,
the snow will pass off with rain; if it is dry inside,
the snow will melt by the sun.

If there is no snow before January,
there will be more snow in March and April.

If the snow melts enough in January so that the bare ground shows in the sugarbush, the following maple sugar season will be poor.

A thunderstorm in February brings an early, wet spring; therefore it will be a poor sugar year.

There will be as many good runs of sap as there are thaws in January.

Rain will follow river water running on top of ice.

When the snow is wet enough to make a snowman and the clouds are blue-tinged and the mountains turn a reddish brown, the snow will turn to corn and the skiing will be at its best.

If Candlemas Day is bright and clear,
we'll have two winters in the year.

Cold is the night when the stars shine bright.

The squeak of snow will the temperature show.

A ring around the moon, snow coming soon.

Clear moon, frost soon.

A heavy November snow will last till April.

If we do not get our Indian Summer in October
or November, we shall get it in the winter.

If there's spring in winter and winter in spring,
the year won't be good for anything.

A wet January, a wet spring.

A year of snow, a year of plenty.

Snow like meal, snow a great deal.

February fog means a frost in May.

It will be a cold, snowy winter if hair on horses is thick early in the season.

A warm Christmas, a cold Easter.